All About Your Labrador

Contents

Absolutely Labradors! — 2
The positives; The negatives; The adult dog; Life expectancy.

What's In A Name? — 6
The shooting dog; The Labrador today.

Choosing A Labrador — 8
The show dog; The working dog; The pet dog; Male or female?; An older dog; More than one; Signs to look for; A healthy puppy.

Getting Ready — 12
Bed and bedding; Indoor crate; Bowls; Toys; Collar and lead; Identification.

The New Arrival — 14
Collecting your puppy; Settling in; The first night; House rules.

Feeding Your Puppy — 16
Feeding methods; Mealtimes; Bones; Feeding problems.

Caring For Your Labrador — 18
Grooming; Nails; Teeth.

Training Your Labrador — 20
House training; Come; Sit; Down; Lead training; Short and sweet.

The Outside World — 23
Car travel; Other animals.

Exercising Your Labrador — 25
Adult exercise; Swimming; Retrieving.

Having Fun With Your Labrador — 27
Training clubs; New challenges; Showing.

Health Care — 29
Vaccinations; Worming (Roundworm; Tapeworm; Heartworm); Breed specific conditions.

Absolutely Labradors!

Affectionate, intelligent, obedient, willing, kind and, above all cheerful. These are the characteristics that have made the Labrador Retriever the most popular breed in Britain and the United States.

If you want to know more about its background and character, and how to choose, care for and train a Labrador, then this is the book for you.

Is the Lab the right dog for you? As you might expect with a breed that has won so many fans, the Labrador's good points far outweigh the bad. Nevertheless, you should consider both advantages and disadvantages very carefully.

THE POSITIVES
Temperament

The Labrador is one of nature's optimists. Bold and friendly, with a love of life, he has an unshakeable belief that however black things may seem, everything will turn out fine in the end. He is naturally affectionate and intelligent with a great sense of fun.

Trainability

Once again, ten out of ten. The Labrador's mix of a good brain and a strong desire to please make it one of the easiest breeds to train.

DID YOU KNOW?

In 1906 Munden Single became the first Labrador to compete in Field Trials. After her death, her body was mounted and is now in a natural history museum in Tring, Hertfordshire, UK.

By nature the Labrador is affectionate and intelligent.

Sociability

Labradors not only like people, they are generally good with other dogs, too. Labs are tolerant and trustworthy with children, and just love to play games. As a family companion the Labrador is second to none, offering devotion, loyalty and good humour.

Maintenance

Well-bred Labradors have few health problems and are generally easy to care for. The short, waterproof coat dries quickly and is easy to keep clean.

THE NEGATIVES
Size

A full grown Labrador is a serious amount of dog, and this combined with a natural exuberance means plenty of living space is required. A Labrador in a small apartment is unlikely to co-exist happily with your priceless collection of antique porcelain. I have witnessed a Lab's tail demolish a trayful of wine glasses with one wag!

Feeding and exercise

The Labrador has yet to be born that knows when it has had enough to eat! Labs will bolt whatever is put in front of them, and are more prone than most breeds to obesity. They also require regular exercise to stay lean and fit.

A strong desire to please makes the Labrador easy to train.

If you are looking for a guard dog, try another breed!

Absolutely Labradors!

Guarding

If you want a reliable guard dog, try another breed. Your Lab is more likely to lick a burglar to death than corner him. However, they do usually bark when anyone approaches the house.

The Adult Dog

Mature males grow to about 23 ins (56 cms) at the withers (top of the shoulder), and weigh 70-75 lbs (32-34 kgs). Bitches are a little shorter in height, measuring 21-22 ins (54 cms), and weighing 55-70 lbs (25-32 kgs).

Labradors may be yellow, black or chocolate in colour. The coat is short and dense, with

Colour is a matter of personal preference.

a weather-resistant undercoat. The 'otter tail' is a distinctive feature of the breed. It should be thick towards the base, gradually tapering towards the tip, clothed thickly all round with short hair, giving it a rounded appearance.

The Labrador was developed as a gundog, and its soft mouth is ideal for picking up and retrieving game.

Life Expectancy

The life expectancy of a Labrador is about twelve years, but it is not uncommon for dogs to reach 14 or 15. So remember that taking on a Labrador is a long-term commitment.

DID YOU KNOW?

In the early days most Labradors were black. The first yellow Labradors appeared in the 1900s.

The Labrador has a good life expectancy – many live to 14 years of age.

What's In A Name

The origins of the Labrador have been extensively researched and there are many differing theories about its beginnings.

However, it is widely believed that the breed came from the East coast of Canada, notably the Newfoundland and St John's area, at the beginning of the 18th century. Black 'water dogs' were used by fishermen to drag nets ashore, and to retrieve fish that had fallen overboard.

Two types existed: one very large, with a heavy coat, which we now recognise as the Newfoundland, and the other, much smaller, known as the St John's dog. It is thought that these two types were crossed with each other to produce a strong, active dog, with a short, weatherproof coat which was ideal for working in water and in cold conditions. From this combination our Labradors are descended.

It has been said the first Labradors reached England some 170 years ago, swimming ashore from the ships which brought fish from Newfoundland. The dogs were known as the St John's breed or "little Newfoundlander" initially, but were renamed 'Labradors' shortly after their integration in England.

The Shooting Dog

In the 1820s, the second Earl of Malmesbury saw dogs playing in the sea and thought they might be suitable for retrieving wildfowl on his estate.

From this beginning, the Labrador was developed as a shooting dog, and its willing, intelligent nature made it

Black 'water dogs' were used to drag fishing nets ashore.

an ideal choice. The third Earl of Malmesbury presented dogs as gifts to other wealthy landowners, and so the breed spread to other large country estates and was soon established as the shooting dog *par excellence*.

The English Kennel Club registered the Labrador as a separate breed in 1904, and by the 1920s the breed was exported to the United States for shooting purposes. It thrived in its new home, and was recognised by the American Kennel Club in the late 1920s.

The Labrador Today

The Labrador remains hugely popular as a working gundog. The combination of a great sense of smell, a biddable temperament, and strong retrieving instincts, makes it invaluable in the field.

The breed's happy and willing nature has led to the development of other important roles. The Labrador is widely used as a guide dog for the blind, and it is becoming increasingly popular as a hearing dog for the deaf and as a dog for the disabled. It has made its mark as a drugs and explosives 'sniffer' dog, and it has brought great benefits in its work as a therapy dog.

The most popular breed used as a guide dog for the blind.

Choosing A Labrador

Whether you want a Labrador as a companion, a show dog, or a shooting dog, it is important to locate breeders with a reputation for producing sound, healthy, good-quality puppies.

The best method is to approach your national kennel club which will be able to put you in touch with the breed club in your area. The breed club secretary will offer advice, and will often know which breeders have puppies for sale.

It is a good plan to visit a Championship dog show, where you will find breeders willing to discuss the Labrador. It is also helpful if you see the different colours, and the different types produced by breeders.

Before you start looking at puppies, it is important to be clear in your own mind as to what you want from your Labrador.

DID YOU KNOW?

The yellow Labrador can vary in shade from pale cream to red fox.

Labrador puppies are irresistible, but keep a clear head when making your choice.

The Show Dog

If you have ambitions to show your dog, you must make your intentions clear so that the breeder can help you to assess the puppies. In this case, it is best to go to a breeder who has been successful in the show ring, and has a wealth of experience in their own breeding lines.

Most breeders will help you to select a show prospect, pointing out whether it has a good head, correct shoulder placement, the correct mouth and dentition, and other breed specifics. However, at eight weeks there is no guarantee a puppy will make the show ring, let alone become a Champion.

The breeder will help you to assess show potential.

The Working Dog

If you require a shooting dog, it is advisable to visit a kennel which predominately produces working stock, and it would be an advantage to observe the mother displaying her ability at retrieving. When selecting a puppy, choose a lively character who is already picking things up and carrying them around.

The Pet Dog

Appearance and retrieving ability are not crucial when you are looking for a pet dog, but it is still important to find a healthy litter of puppies typical of the breed. Temperament is the most important factor to assess.

Male Or Female?

Whether you want a dog or a bitch is very much personal choice.

Bitches tend to be more popular because most people believe they are quieter, and they

DID YOU KNOW?

Scottish gamekeepers went to the USA with their Labradors in the 1920s to help set up shoots.

Choosing A Labrador

There is little difference in temperament between dogs and bitches – but dogs will be bigger and more powerful.

do not grow as large as the males. However, a bitch comes in season twice a year and, unless you plan to neuter, you will have to ensure she is kept away from males during this time. If you decide on neutering, this should be done after the first season.

The male Labrador will be larger and generally more powerful than the female. He can be boisterous as a youngster, and can take a little longer to mature than a bitch, but his personality is just as gentle and devoted.

An Older Dog

You may find in an animal shelter an adult Labrador that needs a new home. This might work out well, but be prepared to give a lot of time and patience to a dog which may have suffered traumas in its earlier life.

More Than One

It is tempting to take on two puppies for the sake of companionship, but, if you want two dogs, it is probably better to leave a minimum twelve-month gap before acquiring your second dog so that you can ensure both receive individual attention and training. If you are planning to keep two Labradors, stick to the same sex as it will lead to fewer problems.

Signs To Look For

When you visit a breeder, take a note on general cleanliness and hygiene, and evidence of happy, healthy, well-groomed dogs. It is helpful if you can see closely-related adults, as this will give an indication of how the puppies may turn out.

Puppies spend a lot of time sleeping, so make sure you see the litter during a playtime before making your choice.

It is essential that you see the mother with her puppies, as this will tell you a lot about temperament. The bitch should appear calm and relaxed, and she should be quite happy to show off her puppies.

Puppies born in a breeder's home and kept there until their eyes are open, are usually are more socialised to household noises than puppies born in a kennel environment

A Healthy Puppy

Look for a healthy puppy displaying alertness, clean, bright eyes, good bones and a clean coat. The puppy should be confident and inquisitive, and ready to come up to greet you. Guard against feeling sorry for the nervous puppy that cowers in a corner – this is a sure sign of unsound temperament.

The breeder will show you a copy of the puppy's pedigree, plus details of hip dysplasia X-ray scores of the parents (see page 31). The parents should also possess current eye certificates stating they are clear of hereditary eye diseases (see page 31). This is of paramount importance.

Getting Ready

Before bringing a new puppy home, make sure you have everything prepared in advance. The area where the puppy is allowed inside the home should be checked for electrical wires, and any other possible hazards. The garden should be made secure, and if you have a swimming pool or a garden pond, it should be fenced off.

Bed And Bedding

Choose a place in the house where you intend your puppy to sleep. The kitchen or utility room is ideal, with the bed located in a corner away from draughts. To start with, a cardboard box, lined with an old blanket or similar soft bedding, will be fine. Alternatively, you can buy a strong plastic bed which is durable and easy to clean. Baskets and bean bags are OK for older Labradors, but they provide a great means of exercising sharp puppy teeth!

Indoor Crate

There is a lot to be said for investing in a collapsible wire crate. This can be used at night-time, and it is also useful for containing your puppy for short periods during the day. The crate will also help with house training, as well as providing a safe means of transporting your dog in the car.

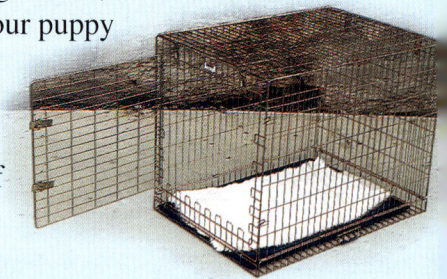

An indoor crate is a wise investment.

Bowls

Your puppy will need its own bowls for food and water. Stainless steel are best. Pottery bowls can break, and plastic ones will be chewed.

Toys

Labrador puppies love toys, and its is a good idea to have a small collection and offer them on a random basis. They should be made of hard rubber, or the fabric 'tugger' type is perfectly safe. Plastic toys belonging to children should be kept out of the way, and old shoes are definitely not recommended. It is impossible for a puppy to differentiate between old shoes and new!

Make sure the toys you choose are tough – and safe.

Collar And Lead

A lightweight collar should be used to begin with so that your Labrador becomes accustomed to having something round his neck. At three months, a more substantial collar and a strong leather lead will be required.

A lightweight collar and lead is suitable for a puppy.

Identification

It is essential that your puppy has some form of identification. This can take the form of a disc or tag attached to the collar, or you may consider having your puppy microchipped. This is a permanent identification, injected by a vet under the skin, in the neck area. It carries a unique number that can be read with a special scanner. If the dog is lost, the details can be traced through a central computer.

The New Arrival

Bringing your Labrador puppy home is a big event for all concerned. For the family, it is a time of great excitement, but for the puppy, it is a bewildering experience to be parted from his littermates and taken to a strange environment. It is your job to make this transition as smooth as possible so that the puppy feels safe and secure.

Bringing your puppy home is a big event for all the family.

Collecting Your Puppy

Let someone else to drive the car so that you can hold your new pet on your lap for the journey home. Bring an old towel or blanket so the puppy will be comfortable.

The breeder should give you a diet sheet, and possibly enough food for the first couple of meals. This helps to keep change to a minimum. The breeder should also hand over the pedigree, and the kennel club registration certificate if it is available. Details of the worming programme should also be supplied.

Settling In

When you arrive home, show your Lab his new bed and general surroundings, and take him to the garden to relieve himself. You can then offer a meal, but do not be surprised if the puppy feels too overwhelmed to eat.

Allow your puppy to settle in quietly, and, if

you have children, make sure they do not get too excited. They must realise that a puppy needs a great deal of sleep.

The First Night

This can be a traumatic experience for the owner as well as the puppy. Naturally, your Labrador feels he has been abandoned, and he will cry for attention. A radio playing quietly can help the 'settling in' process, but usually a trip down to the kitchen in the middle of the night is necessary to offer comfort.

Your puppy may feel bewildered to begin with.

House Rules

Make sure that your Labrador knows what is expected of him right from the start. He should know which areas of the house or garden are out of bounds, and these rules should always be applied.
• Going up and down stairs puts strain on growing bones and joints, so it is better if your Lab is not allowed upstairs.
• Begging at the table is a bad habit, and should be discouraged.
• Jumping up should be stopped at an early stage, as this can be positively dangerous when your puppy develops into a big, strong adult.

DID YOU KNOW?

The Labrador, with its highly developed sense of smell, has been used to locate victims of earthquakes buried under tons of rubble.

Feeding Your Labrador

Whatever feeding method you choose, make sure the diet you provide is of the highest quality. A Labrador's growth-rate is at its maximum between eight weeks and five months, and so it is essential to feed a correctly balanced diet during this period in order to produce a fit and healthy dog.

Feeding Methods

Some breeders prefer the traditional method, which involves feeding meat or tripe and biscuits, alternating with milk and cereal, plus vitamins. Nowadays there are many different types of 'complete diet' available. These have been tested for nutritional balance, and they have proved excellent for rearing puppies. Make sure you follow the manufacturer's feeding instructions, and ensure that fresh water is always available.

It is important that no other food or vitamins is added to a complete diet as this destroys the nutritional balance.

Whichever method of feeding you choose, it is wise to stick to the diet the breeder used for the first few weeks. If you wish to make a change, do so gradually, over a period of days.

DID YOU KNOW?

It takes two decades for the adult human skeleton to develop. With a Labrador, all the growth development is compressed into twelve months.

Mealtimes

- 8 to 12 weeks: Feed four times a day.
- 12 weeks to 5 months: Feed three times a day.
- 5 to 11 months: Feed twice a day.

Once a Labrador is a year old some people prefer to feed just one meal a day, while others prefer to divide the ration into two meals. This is up to you – but do beware of over-feeding. Learn to resist those pleading eyes!

Bones

A marrow bone (sawn, not chopped as this can splinter) is beneficial for a puppy, particularly at around sixteen weeks when he is teething. An artificial bone, such as Nylabone, is even safer. Hide chews are also suitable. Make sure your Labrador is supervised when he has a bone, and do not allow him to become possessive over it.

Feeding Problems

Occasionally, a puppy may refuse a meal. If this happens, remove the bowl, and offer fresh food at the next mealtime. If your Labrador suffers from diarrhoea, offer fish, chicken or rice. If the problem persists for more than 24 hours, or the motions contain blood, seek veterinary advice.

It is essential to feed a well-balanced diet during the growing period.

Caring For Your Labrador

DID YOU KNOW?

The colouring of a chocolate Labrador may be affected with exposure to sunshine.

The Labrador is a low-maintenance breed, but it is important to keep a regular check on general health and well-being.

Grooming

The new owner needs basic grooming equipment. This should include

- A stiff brush
- A steel comb
- A chamois leather
- A pair of nail-clippers.

It is a good idea to brush your Labrador regularly – twice a week, or more if you wish – making sure it is always a pleasurable experience. Use a comb for removing dead hair, which is particularly important when your dog is shedding his coat. With bitches this occurs twice a year, usually about twelve weeks after being in season. A male sheds his coat once a year, often in the Spring with the onset of warm weather.

A chamois leather can be used after grooming to give your dog's coat that special shine.

Accustom your puppy to being groomed from an early age.

No matter how careful you are, your Labrador may occasionally pick up fleas. There are a variety of preventative measures that you can take, so it is best to ask your vet for advice.

Nails

Examine your puppy's toenails regularly as these grow quickly if he is not being exercised on hard surfaces. If the nails are too long, they should be cut using a pair of nail-clippers. This is a relatively simple task, but ask your vet to show you how to do it the first time. It is important not to cut into the quick as this will cause the nail to bleed.

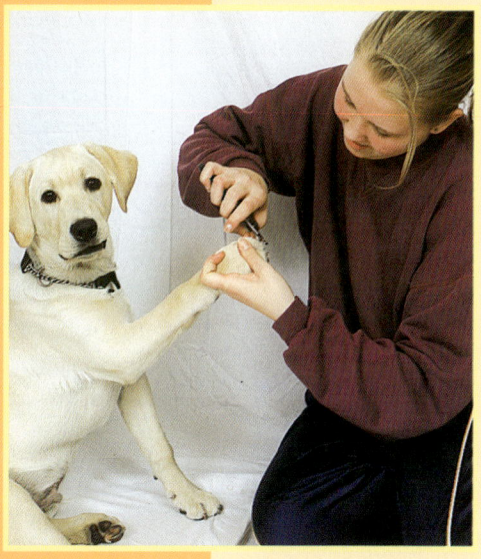

Nails must be kept in trim.

Teeth

Teeth should be checked, and if a marrow bone or hide chew is not provided regularly, they can be kept clean with the use of a toothbrush and canine toothpaste. This will help to prevent the build up of tartar and eliminate bad breath.

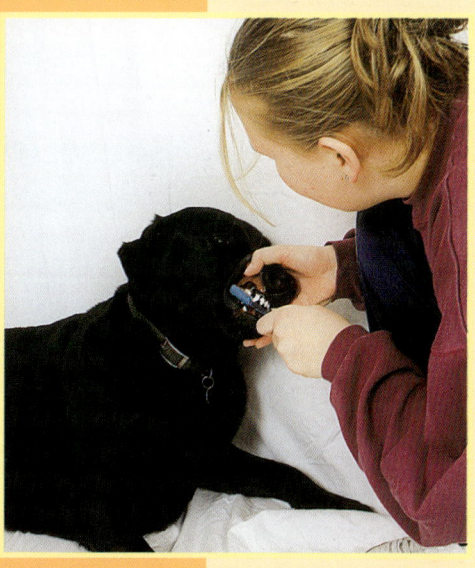

Teeth and gums will stay healthy with regular cleaning.

Training Your Labrador

It is never too early to begin training. The golden rules are to start as you mean to go on, and to be firm, fair and consistent. Your Lab will soon learn the meaning of "No", but make sure you are just as quick to offer praise when he does something right. A young Labrador learns from the tone of your voice, and with plenty of love and understanding, he will soon become settled and accustomed to his new life.

The sooner you start training, the better.

DID YOU KNOW?

A dog called Buccleuch Avon, bred by Lord Malmesbury in 1885, is believed to be the ancestor of all black Labradors.

House Training

The first lesson for your Labrador to learn is to be clean in the house. Allocate an area of your garden, and take him to this spot every time he needs to relieve himself. This will be after he has eaten, after a sleep, and after a game. Wait until he has performed, give praise, and bring him back in. Many owners find a command, such as "Be clean" is a useful aid.

Come

Your Labrador should learn right from the start to come when he is called. When he is settling into his new home he will be only too willing to respond, so work on this by using his name, followed by the command "Come" or "Here". Call him in a friendly, persuasive tone of voice, and reward with praise and a food treat.

Sit

Teaching a Labrador to sit is one of the simplest exercises. If you hold a treat above his head, he will naturally go into the sit position. As he does this, give the command, and then reward with praise and the treat. The same procedure can be followed at mealtimes.

Hold a treat above your puppy's head, and as he looks up, he will naturally go into the Sit position.

Down

This should be taught as an extension of the sit exercise. When your Labrador is sitting, lower a treat to the ground, and he will follow it into the down position. Give the command as he goes into position, and reward with the treat. Work on your timing, so that the dog associates the command with what he is doing

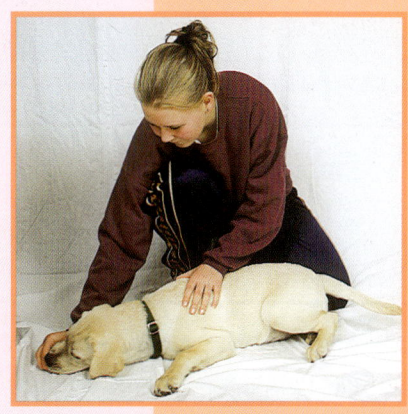

Lower the treat to the floor, and the puppy will go into the Down.

Training Your Labrador

Lead Training

This is very important – there is nothing worse than an 80 lb Labrador pulling its owner down the road.

Attach the lead, and, to begin with, follow your Labrador where he wants to go. The next step is to encourage him to follow you. Give lots of praise, and do not be too harsh with correction. When your Labrador is walking by your side, use the command "Heel". If he pulls ahead, bring him back to your side, and only give the command when he is in the correct position.

> **DID YOU KNOW?**
>
> In the Second World War, Labradors were used for detecting land mines, reputedly accomplishing the work with more speed than any other breed.

Practise lead training at home before venturing into the outside world.

Short And Sweet

Never make training sessions too long when a Labrador is young – up to ten minutes a day is ample. Always end the session on a happy, positive note, praising your dog and finishing with a game.

The Outside World

Labrador puppies must complete a full vaccination course before they are allowed to venture into the outside world (see page 29).

This marks the start of a new and exciting time in his life. He will, of course, have met visitors in your home, but now he will be faced with a wide variety of different experiences. Fortunately, Labradors are out-going and friendly, and, in most cases, you will be coping with over-exuberance rather than nervousness.

Be firm at all times, and do not allow your Labrador to pull on the lead or to jump up. If he is worried about anything, do not make a big deal of it. If you make too much of a fuss, the dog will think there really is cause for concern!

Most Labrador puppies will take new situations in their stride.

Car Travel

The earlier your Labrador begins to travel by car, the less likelihood there is of car sickness occurring. It can be beneficial to allow him to sit in a stationary car for a few minutes at a time. Labradors usually enjoy travelling and soon learn to sit quietly. The safest way to transport your dog is in a crate fitted in the rear of the car.

Remember, *never* leave a dog in a car on a hot day – even in shade, the temperature can rise very quickly and this can be fatal.

The Outside World

Other Animals

Meeting other animals is an important part of socialisation. Make sure that all introductions are closely supervised, preferably with your Labrador on a lead. If he makes any attempt to bark or to chase livestock, this must be instantly curbed.

The well-socialised puppy exposed to a wide variety of different experiences will learn to take all new situations in his stride.

Exercising Your Labrador

It is a very common mistake for Labrador owners to over-exercise their puppies, and this can lead to serious problems. It is important to understand that a dog's bones do not calcify until approximately seven to eight months of age. Therefore, damage can result if bones and joints are over-taxed.

Playing in the garden is adequate, but once a puppy has been inoculated he needs to go out and socialise. By three months of age, your puppy can go for a quiet walk on the lead for about a quarter of a mile. This can be stepped up gradually, combining it with some free-running exercise by the age of six months.

Adult Exercise

Most Labradors need space to release their energy and adore exercise over fields or running through woods where they can use their noses. Obviously, you must ensure that your dog is allowed to free-run in that area, and you must be confident that he is under your control.

Road exercise is excellent for building hard muscle and it helps to keep the feet and nails in good shape.

The amount of exercise needed varies from dog to dog. The ideal routine for most Labradors is an hour free-running in the morning and a short evening walk, as well as being let out in the garden during the course of the day.

Exercising Your Labrador

Swimming

Bearing in mind the Labrador was originally a 'water dog', you will discover that most members of the breed have a passion for swimming. Not only is this great for muscle building, it also helps to keep the coat clean and removes dead hair when moulting. Make sure you choose a safe place for swimming where there are no strong currents.

Labradors have a natural affinity with water.

Retrieving

Labradors love to retrieve, and this is a useful form of exercise. Make sure you use a safe 'retrieve toy' rather than allowing your dog to retrieve a stick, which can prove hazardous.

Watch out for the inevitable shake!

Having Fun With Your Labrador

The Labrador is an intelligent, adaptable dog, and is willing to take on many different tasks. Both dog and owner can derive enormous pleasure in anything from involvement in an obedience training club to the exhilaration of competing in working trials, agility or gundog tests, or taking on the challenge of the show ring.

Training Clubs

It is important to find a good training club. Initially, it is best to go alone to check out the methods of instruction, and to find out if training takes place in a happy, positive atmosphere. To start with, your Labrador will be taught the basic commands of sit and stay, heel on a lead, recall and retrieve.

You may wish to try Competitive Obedience with your Labrador.

Having Fun With Your Labrador

New Challenges
Assuming your Labrador progresses well, he may be ready to have a go at Competitive Obedience, or try Working Trials, which combine the disciplines of obedience, tracking and agility. For those with a working dog, the discipline of Field Trials provides a tremendous challenge.

Agility has gained rapidly in popularity, and it now has a worldwide following. It is best described as an obstacle course comprising jumps, hurdles, tunnels (soft canvas type) see-saw, and weaving poles, and the dog has to complete the course in the fastest time. This is a fun sport for both dog and owner, and although Labradors are not as quick as some breeds, such as Border Collies, they have proved highly successful in this area.

Showing
Showing can be a very rewarding hobby. If you have a Labrador of show quality, you will both need to attend special training classes so that you know what is required in the ring. Start off at a small show, and if you are successful you can work your way up the scale. You may even make your dog a Champion.

Health Care

Labradors are a healthy, hardy breed, and suffer few health problems. However, it is essential that you keep up-to-date with both vaccination and worming programmes.

Vaccinations

All puppies must be vaccinated to protect them against several potentially fatal diseases.

These are : -

Distemper (also known as hardpad).
Infectious hepatitis, a liver disease.
Parvovirus, which causes acute gastro-enteritis.
Leptospirosis. There are two forms, contracted from rodents, that cause liver or kidney failure.
Rabies. This is a viral disease that is transmittable to all mammals, including man. The UK is free of rabies due to its long-standing quarantine policy, but dogs living elsewhere need to be vaccinated against the disease.

The exact timing of the vaccinations depends on the particular vaccine used, and your vet will advise you. Most involve a first injection at any time from eight weeks of age, with a second at twelve weeks. Your Labrador will need a regular booster injection each year.

Health Care

Worming

Your Labrador should have been wormed by the breeder, and it is advisable to continue with a regular worming programme indefinitely. Your vet will advise you.

Worms which may affect your Labrador are:

ROUNDWORM

Puppies are usually infected with roundworm from their mother. Roundworm can cause problems if ingested by children, and in extreme cases can affect their eyesight, so it is essential that your dog is kept clear.

TAPEWORM

Occasionally a Labrador may be infested with tapeworm. This long, flat worm lives within the intestine, with its head firmly anchored. Rice-like segments break off from the end of the worm, and can be seen in the faeces, or, more commonly, stuck to the hair around the dog's anal region.

HEARTWORM

This parasite lives in the heart and can cause significant problems. The intermediate host is the mosquito and so dogs living in tropical areas are more likely to be affected. If you live in an area where heartworm is endemic, it is essential to adopt a worming programme.

Breed Specific Conditions

The Labrador is a relatively large, heavy dog, and so bones and joints are vulnerable, particularly during the growing period. Hip dysplasia and osteochondrosis are both diseases with an hereditary basis, but they can also be influenced by environment.

The incidence of hip dysplasia, a chronic and painful condition which affects the hip joints, has been reduced considerably by ensuring that breeding stock is free of the disease. This is done by a process called hip scoring. Different methods are used in different countries, but your vet will explain the procedure

An eye condition known as entropion, where the eyelids turn inwards, can affect the Labrador. The early signs of this are excessive watering of the eyes. This condition can be corrected with surgery. Progressive Retinal Atrophy (PRA), is an eye disease resulting in blindness which can only be diagnosed in adulthood.

It is essential that all Labradors used for breeding are eye-tested and pronounced clear of hereditary eye diseases.